GUITAR PRELUDES

BY WILLIAM BAY

ISBN 978-09888327-2-5

© 2013 BY WILLIAM BAY
ALL RIGHTS RESERVED. INTERNATIONAL COPYRIGHT SECURED. B.M.I.

Visit us on the Web at www.williambaymusic.com

PREFACE

The guitar is such a wonderfully expressive instrument. The various possibilities available for tone color, timbre, voicings, etc. make composing for guitar a joyous task and also a challenge. I wrote these preludes to provide concert or recital material for the plectrum guitarist. They reflect an interesting variety of rhythms, keys, moods and harmonies.

The tempo markings are suggestions. The pieces should be played at tempos that feel comfortable and natural to you.

I have always believed that the plectrum or flatpick guitar could be an exciting concert instrument. It is with this in mind that I have written and recorded numerous items in the **William Bay Music** catalog. These items may be found on my website; *williambaymusic.com*.

I hope you enjoy playing these pieces as much as I enjoyed composing them!

William Bay

CONTENTS

Prelude #1 in A minor	4
Prelude #2 in C Major	7
Prelude #3 in D minor	10
Prelude #4 in A Major	14
Prelude #5 in B minor	17
Prelude #6 in G Major	20
Prelude #7 in E minor	24
Prelude #8 in C♯ minor	29
Prelude #9 in E Major	32
Prelude #10 in F♯ minor	36
Prelude #11 in D Major	40
Prelude #12 in A minor	44
Prelude #13 in A Major	48
Prelude #14 in D minor	52
Prelude #15 in C minor	56

PRELUDE I/ A MINOR

William Bay

PRELUDE 2/ C MAJOR

Lyrically ♩. = 66

William Bay

*Finger note with r.h. index finger and pluck note with r.h. thumb.

PRELUDE 3/ D MINOR

13

PRELUDE 4/ A MAJOR

Lively Tempo ♩=66

William Bay

PRELUDE 5/ B MINOR

William Bay

PRELUDE 6/ G MAJOR

* Finger note with R.H. index finger and pluck with R.H. thumb.

PRELUDE 7/ E MINOR

William Bay

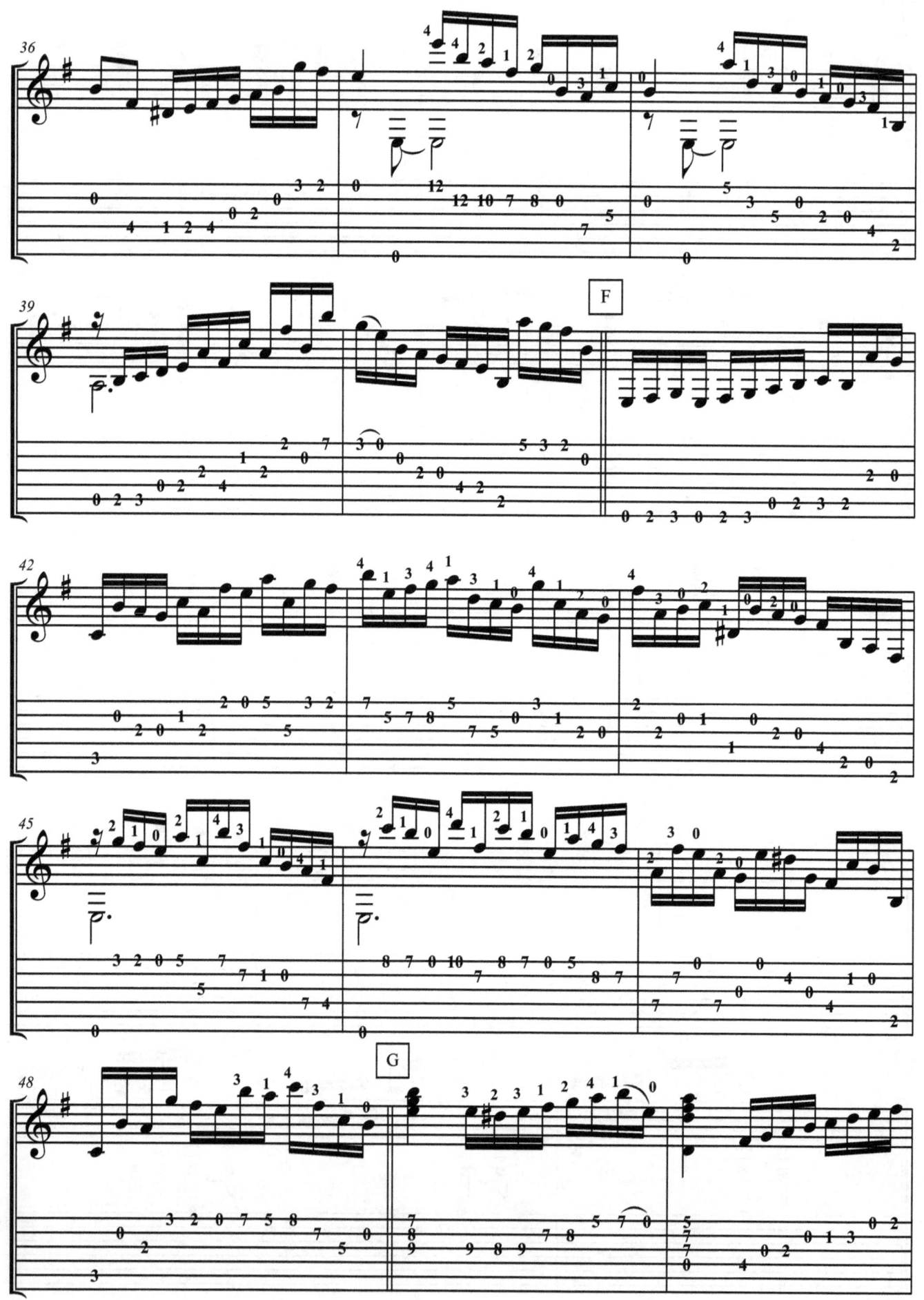

PRELUDE 8/ C# MINOR

William Bay

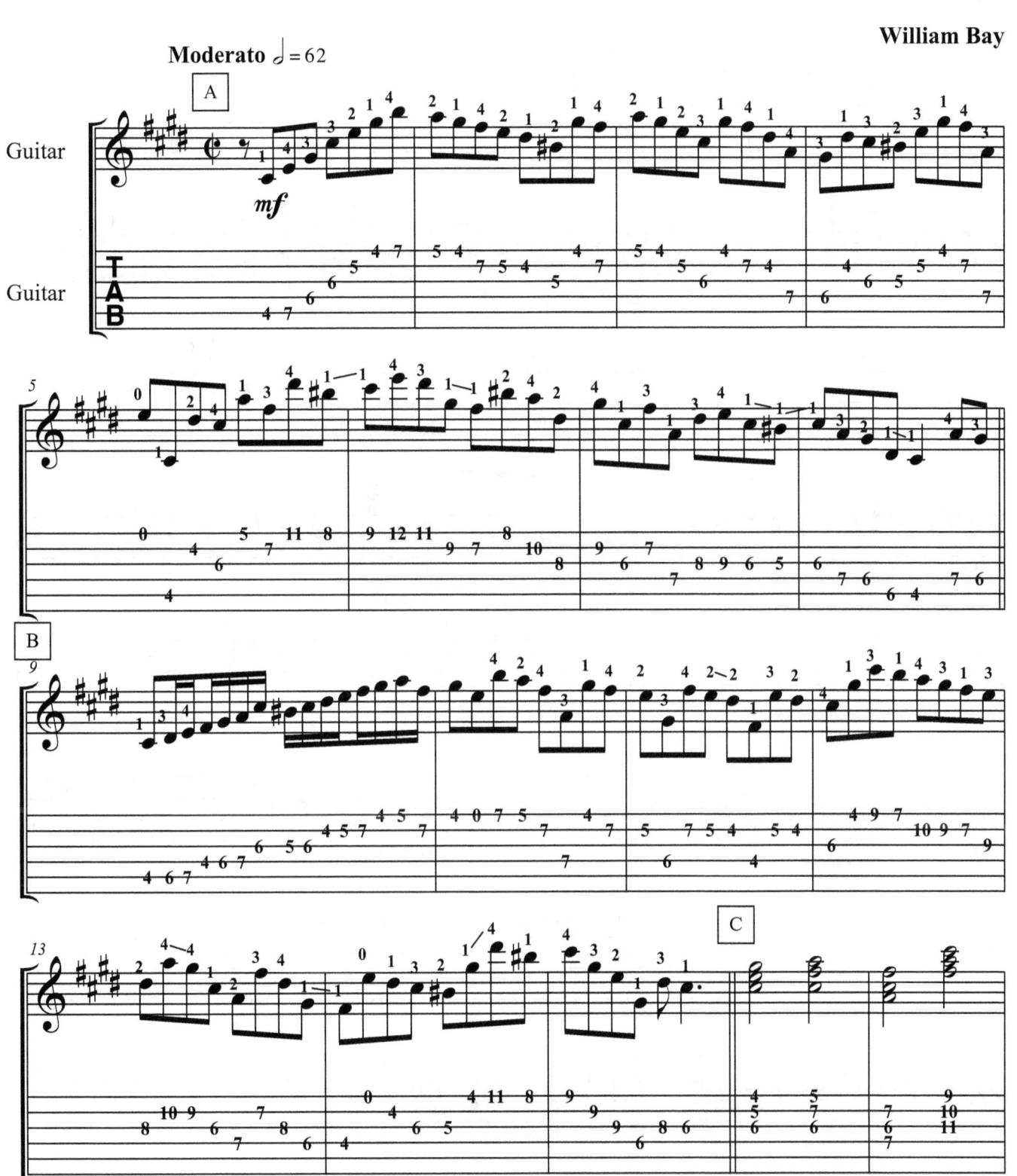

PRELUDE 9/ E MAJOR

William Bay

PRELUDE 10/ F# MINOR

39

PRELUDE II / D MAJOR

Dropped D Tuning

William Bay

41

PRELUDE 12/ A MINOR

William Bay

© 2013 by William Bay. All Rights Reserved. BMI.

This page has been left blank to avoid awkward page turns.

PRELUDE 13/ A MAJOR

William Bay

Joyfully ♩.=68

PRELUDE 14/ D MINOR

Dropped D Tuning

Slowly ♩ = 100

William Bay

© 2013 by William Bay. All Rights Reserved. BMI.

This page has been left blank
to avoid awkward page turns.

PRELUDE 15 / C MINOR

Allegro ♩ = 100

William Bay

WWW.WILLIAMBAYMUSIC.COM

www.ingramcontent.com/pod-product-compliance
Lightning Source LLC
LaVergne TN
LVHW061256060426
835507LV00020B/2331